I'm Here, I'm Here!

A little book about my BIG first year

I'm Here, I'm Here!

A little book about my BIG first year

by Valerie Carlson Pressley
Illustrated by Kayla Lynn Olson

ABOOKS
Alive Book Publishing

I'm Here, I'm Here!
Copyright © 2020 by Valerie Carlson Pressley
Illustrations by Kayla Lynn Olson

Additional copies may be ordered from the publisher
for educational, business, promotional or premium use.
For information, contact ALIVE Book Publishing at:
alivebookpublishing.com, or call (925) 837-7303.

ISBN 13
978-1-63132-095-8

Library of Congress Control Number: 2020910519

Library of Congress Cataloging-in-Publication Data
is available upon request.

First Edition

Published in the United States of America
by ALIVE Book Publishing
an imprint of Advanced Publishing LLC
3200 A Danville Blvd., Suite 204, Alamo, California 94507
alivebookpublishing.com

PRINTED IN THE UNITED STATES OF AMERICA

10 9 8 7 6 5 4 3 2 1

For Georgia and Logan

I'm here, I'm here! A baby so dear.
A new cutie to cuddle and hold so near.

I'm growing and changing
with each passing day.
I need help doing everything,
but that's okay.

I can lift my head quite high in the sky,
to watch knees and feet
as they shuffle by.

I do my best to gently gurgle and coo.
And can master a quick game
of peek-a-boo.

I love to smile and make funny faces.
I can fit on your lap,
and in lots of small spaces.

I show off my tricks,
like grabbing my toes.
And what I'll do next,
no one really knows.

I clap when I'm happy,
and clap just because.
It's fun to be praised
with smooches and hugs.

I like to roll over,
and have started to crawl.
I'm thinking of walking soon,
but don't want to fall.

I'm getting so big now;
I'm almost One year!
Not really a baby anymore,
but have no fear.

I will wave bye-bye and blow a big kiss,
because turning One is something
I don't want to miss!

Also by Valerie Carlson Pressley

I'm Here, I'm Here!
I'm One, I'm One!
I'm Two, I'm Two!

ABOOKS

ALIVE Book Publishing and ALIVE Publishing Group
are imprints of Advanced Publishing LLC,
3200 A Danville Blvd., Suite 204, Alamo, California 94507

Telephone: 925.837.7303
alivebookpublishing.com

.